# SURVIVE TO THRIVE

# SURVIVE TO THRIVE

*A Practical Guide*
*for the New Network Marketer*

**JAY MAYMI**

iUniverse, Inc.
Bloomington

# SURVIVE TO THRIVE
## A Practical Guide for the New Network Marketer

*iUniverse books may be ordered through booksellers or by contacting:*

*iUniverse*
*1663 Liberty Drive*
*Bloomington, IN 47403*
*www.iuniverse.com*
*1-800-Authors (1-800-288-4677)*

*ISBN: 978-1-4697-4014-0 (sc)*
*ISBN: 978-1-4697-4015-7 (ebk)*

*Printed in the United States of America*

*iUniverse rev. date: 02/17/2012*

# REVIEWER'S COMMENTARY OF "SURVIVE TO THRIVE"

"Jay Maymi has written an excellent primer for beginning Network-Marketers and Direct Sellers. His chapter on 'Master the Words' is worth the entire book, but you'll get so much more from the other chapters as well. I highly recommend this book!"

- *MJ Durkin, Author of Double Your Contacts.*

"Jay has a unique style of introducing practical thoughts which can be applied immediately into your organization. His many years of being in the trenches have taught him valuable lessons which you will be blessed to learn through reading this book. In our world of independence and self-reliance, Jay poses an insight on how to minimize your mistakes and maximize your learning curve. As a minister and fellow networker I found Jay's spiritual understanding to be very inspirational giving great perspective that there is a God that desires for us to be successful."

- *Rev. Frank Hines, Founder and Director,*
  *Charity Wellness Center*

"This is definitely a great read and applicable to anyone in network marketing who desires to cultivate the right mentality. The writing style is conversational which provides an easy, quick, and informative read. I would recommend it."

- *Fradel Barber, Executive Marketing Director, World Financial Group*

"This book can only be written by someone doing it!"

- *Bill Mitchell, Executive Vice Chairman, World Financial Group*

"If I was venturing into something new that involved both risk and reward, I would want to minimize my risk and maximize my reward. This book will do just that! It will guide any network marketer past the initial stumbling blocks and onto a massively successful business career."

- *Chris Philippi, Co-Author of "Create The Business Breakthrough You Want"*

# ACKNOWLEDGEMENTS

First, I would like to give thanks to God for the abilities and talents He gives me to create such a project. It is always an honor and a privilege to use these gifts to impact, inspire and make a difference in someone else's life.

As anyone who has ever undertaken the task of producing a project of this scale knows, it is never an individual effort. There are always others who work behind the scenes tirelessly and diligently in making the final product worthwhile. As such, I would like to give special recognition to my wife Ivette, who provides not only the editorial support but the moral support as well. This is truly a team effort! In addition, I want to thank my children Cailyn, Keanu and Caleb, who provide all of the cheerleading a father could ever want.

Finally, a special thanks to all of my business colleagues, teammates, and mentors over the years that have helped me to develop and refine as a leader. I would also like to thank Chris Philippi and Joe Maymi for providing the early guidance and insight I needed. It was greatly appreciated.

# PREFACE

**W**ell, congratulations! You've made a decision that so many never make. The decision to build your own business is one that can have incredible life-altering ramifications for you and your family. While just about everyone dreams of being in business for themselves few ever take that leap of faith, garner sufficient courage, or believe in themselves enough to boldly go where they've never been before. Now that you have done the hardest part (decided to go for it), what has changed? Did your name change? Has your wallet been stolen? Is your home or apartment no longer there? Did your kids disappear or move out? (I know what some of you are thinking. Stop that.) Are you better looking or still as ugly as ever? Or has your hair grown back? (As I wish were the case with me!) Of course, none of these things occurred. Yet, here's what did change . . . the possibilities of winning became a reality. Your destiny has potentially taken a turn for the better. You've open the door for blessing and financial gain to pay you a visit. Financial freedom, stress-free living, security, and the privilege of controlling your own time are now in play and can be yours in the not too distant future. You can pull out the scratch pad (or IPad) and begin designing your goals and dreams or blow the dust off the old ones. That's what has changed. Not a bad thing whatsoever and all because you made a decision to go for it. To give it a good, honest try. It's truly amazing what this courageous, yet seemingly small and insignificant decision that an overwhelming number of people never arrive at, can lead to. I am genuinely excited for you and hope for you the best in your business. My sincerest desire is that you make it and become yet another winning example for us to point to. Your success will validate, once again, to our friends, family, colleagues, and the general public at large that our industry works, our business models have credibility, and that making a decision to step outside your comfort zone and do something incredibly special is well worth the effort and does create tremendous value for everyone. So, let me congratulate you once again. Now, let's learn how to survive the business long enough to thrive in your business.

# INTRODUCTION

**D**on't look for the million dollar home. You won't find it. In fact, it would take you less than 5 minutes to tour my residence. Forget finding a Benz, a BMW, or Porsche in the driveway. Been there done that. A boat is something I have never owned and it's not because I don't swim very well. My clothing? Well, I'm not much of a stylist but I do like to wear nice outfits and good suits just as long as they are priced right. The only jewelry I wear is my wedding ring and a silver necklace my mom got me twenty one years ago for my 21st birthday (I've never taken it off). Not quite the lavish lifestyle that you would come to expect from an experienced business owner who is writing a book about establishing the necessary early mindset needed to survive and thrive in your own business or career. However, if you measure success by the size of your home, the type of car you drive, whether you own a boat, expensive clothing, or jewelry then you have missed it by a mile. These are all wonderful things to own or strive for, and yes they do put on display tangible signs of the type of success that most aspire to achieve. However, success is truly relative. It is specifically and uniquely defined by the one person who is determined to find it. You. As a former employee in social services, success for me has been defined by, not just the material things, but also the fact that I have enjoyed the freedom that I never would have if I remained at a job.

I have learned that you cannot put a price on the luxury that freedom affords you over your time, decisions, and life. There are many who do own a lot of these wonderful aforementioned items but lack the freedom to enjoy them. My children have learned first hand that life will give you what you are willing to fight for and also what you are willing to accept. That life lesson is priceless.

As I write this book, I am still in hot pursuit of my ever increasing business goals and personal dreams because as I achieve one I replace it with another. My business continues to steadily grow even through some rough times. As a result, over the last twenty years my compensation has surpassed my salary as a previous social services employee by tenfold. On my previous salary, I would have had to work 60 plus years to earn the money I've earned in just the last fifteen years. An amount of money that, although not as much as other incredibly more successful individuals in business, I would have never seen or would have had the chance to experience had I remained at a job. The places that I have been able to visit around the world due to contests and prizes that we have been blessed to win are places that so many only dream of visiting. For instance, on a social worker's salary, I would have had to save for years just to have been able to take my family to Hawaii one time yet I've been there (and to many of the islands) seven times and have stayed at the most luxurious resorts. I have been able to do so many extremely cool things to help others who were in need, contribute to charities and bless ministries, eaten at some of the best restaurants worldwide, seen fantastic shows, associated with incredible people, and expose my family to amazing experiences. I am in an elite league of industry entrepreneurs to have made a consistent six figure income in one company and then do it again consistently in another. It's a feat that many never achieve. My office walls display awards and recognition paraphernalia that I have been given consistently for years. They showcase a track record of success and a history of achievement. The crowds that I have been honored and privileged to address have ranged from a few to over 30,000. I have recruited, trained, coached and led a few thousand (and counting) entrepreneurs over my twenty year career. There have been countless of lives that I have positively impacted as either business associates or clients, as well. Now, for someone who grew up in the hood in the Spanish Harlem section (El Barrio) of NYC and boasts no extraordinary academic skills, achievements, or grades throughout high school or college, this is success relative to me. In my relentless pursuit for a greater level of achievement and a higher stage of success, I remain humble in knowing that there is still more for me to learn, grow, and accomplish.

So, why this book? Why would this survival guide be of benefit to you? What could you stand to gain from it that can have an immediate impact on the most crucial part of building the initial mindset needed to win big in your business? What is so vital for you to understand as you launch your business that can help you survive your ever so critical first year? Before I answer those very important questions, let's first take a look at what this book is not. This book is not another motivational book filled with stories, catchy phrases, or clichés to temporarily inflate you with awe, excitement, and hype. If you are looking for that type of material then put this book back or don't even purchase it. Those books are great and should be read by every person looking for inspiration and real life lessons. However, many of the people who read them never do the things necessary to change their circumstance. The motivation lasts until they stop at the red light on their way home from the motivational event they have just attended or completed the CD or book they were drawn into. This book is not is a rehash of other self-help books, coaching series, motivational tapes, or seminars. It is the real life, in the trenches, business experience of someone who has been there and done that and continues to until this day. Although there is something to be said about speakers and authors of self-help material, or selling and recruiting instructional books, most have never really done any of what they speak about. It is almost like reading an instructional book from a doctor about performing difficult surgeries yet the doctor has never performed actual surgeries before. He or she has just been a spectator looking in on the surgeries, or interviewing practicing surgeons, or basically summarizing or rehashing other doctors' instructional materials. Only an experienced doctor who has performed surgery after surgery can truly detail with authenticity the experience of his practice. Only someone who has been hands-on can provide real time guidance, a credible roadmap, and skill set development to properly prepare another budding young eager surgeon. Let me propose this point in another way. You have been given a birthday card which contains a gift certificate to have a one hour charter plane tour of the Grand Canyon. Naturally, you are excited about the experience. Upon your arrival, you check in and find out that the weather is a bit rough. There is some light rain and the winds are blowing harder than normal but not sufficient enough to cancel the flight tour. As you sit in the lobby waiting to board the plane, you see a number of pamphlets and instructional guides about flying a charter plane over the Grand Canyon. It appears they are all authored by the same individual and seem very well written and knowledgeable. Then, all of a sudden a tour personnel comes out and announces that the pilot scheduled for the tour will not be making it and they have a substitute to take his place. As the substitute is introduced you notice that it is the same guy from the instructional brochures that you were just reading. As the substitute pilot is giving instructions to the group, you overhear that it is his first time ever in the cockpit flying a charter plane. In fact, upon further inquiry you discover that he does not even have a pilot's license and has never logged flight time! So, my question to you would be, "how fast would you reschedule your tour for another day when the qualified and experienced pilot is back?" The answer would be . . . immediately! Why? Is it because you believe that the substitute pilot is not knowledgeable or well informed about flying? Not quite. Is it because he is incapable of giving you hard nose facts about flying a charter plane over the Grand Canyon? No. Not all. It is because he has never logged flight time! He's never flown a charter plane much less in uncooperative weather conditions. His written material may be superb but he lacks the hands-on seasoning that only occurs when you've actually performed the task that you write or talk about. So many of the material that exists in today's marketplace for the entrepreneur is outstanding and should be utilized as additional resources for skill set development, self improvement, and motivation but only an experienced individual will bring the rich and insightful perspective that new business builders can confidently rely on and make applicable when growing their businesses. This book is just that book. It is written from a variety of personal experiences from recruiting and training thousands over my twenty year career. It is a seasoned and in-depth book that comes from an enormous amount of achievements, setbacks, mistakes, and progress.

The context of this book could only have been written by someone who has logged flight time. A lot of flight time. The context is not re-worded, summarized, or a clever regurgitation of multiple other sources. You will find none of that here. What you will find is tried and true counsel that will help prepare you, substantively, for your entry into our industry. Regardless, what company or business model you are a part of there are a number of mindset fundamentals that you need to establish right now, that will determine whether you survive and thrive or just plain die.

This book was written with the intent of helping you not die within the first year of your business. There. I could not have said it any plainer. The unfortunate reality is that many enthusiastic, wide-eyed, and hopeful new associates join a business because they sincerely intend on making it work. They see it as the shot that they had been looking for to achieve a level of success that can change their circumstances. A noble and genuine motive for entry. However, somewhere along the way, this once excited and vibrant person begins to wane in ambition, enthusiasm, and desire. Focus is lost and before long they have been lost to the witness protection program. For many leaders and team builders this can be one of those great mysteries of the universe not to mention frustrating as hell. In this scenario, no one wins. Not the new associate. Not the manager. Not the company. Certainly, not the client who would have benefited from the product or service had the new associate stayed around long enough to present it to them. So what actually happens? In my opinion, the new associate was never really prepped and equipped with the initial mindset that needed to be established and implemented in order for him/her to survive. You have to survive the business long enough to build a business. I believe that it is vital to train a new associate on making warm market phone calls, communication and language development, understanding product and service features, giving effective presentations, recruiting, closing sales, and on and on, but by itself will not enhance the new associates chances of survival. You see, knowing these things are important but if you don't make it past the first few months then none of it matters. These particular skill sets must be mastered to become successful, it's true. However, they are skill sets that can take time to develop effectively and unfortunately too many quit too soon to ever see their skill sets mature and become profitable. Somewhere along the way, another unsuspected dynamic occurred that derailed their excitement, hopes, and dreams. This precious new associate never saw it coming. They were blindsided because a series of very critical survival tactics were never brought to his/her attention and they proved to be the business death of them. The most important training that you can go through as you enter into this arena is the mindset you develop in order to survive. Without question, there are absolute land mines as you get started in building your own network marketing business. These land mines are never visible and without a guide you can end up blowing yourself up. The great news is that if you can get past these initial land mines (relatively unscathed) then you are on your way. It is my sincerest hope that this book becomes for you (and your future business colleagues as well) the survival guide that equips you with the necessary information to help you survive and thrive in your network marketing business. Over the next ten chapters, I encourage you to become a student of these helpful pointers and apply them often. You will develop the necessary foundational mindset that will take your business past survival and into the realm of the success that you initially signed up for.

# CHAPTER 1

*"The difference between a successful person and others is not lack of strength, not lack of knowledge, but rather a lack in will."*

Vince Lombardi

## "DROP THE ANCHOR"

Anchors serve to keep large sailing vessels from losing their position once they have docked. It provides the stability the boat needs in order to remain in its intended location. Incidentally, the bigger the vessel the bigger the anchor must be. Without good anchoring, a sailing vessel could easily find itself being tossed about and drifting further away from where it is supposed to be due to strong winds, high tides, powerful waves and a number of other factors. The occurrence of this situation can present any captain and his crew incredible frustration, undue stress, repetitious work, and in worse case scenarios, altering plans altogether. Although the analogy I am giving you pertains to the anchors on a ship or a boat, if you are going to survive and thrive then you will also need good anchoring to avoid the similar consequences mentioned above. The good anchoring I am referring to will keep you in your business so that when the strong winds of doubt rage in, the high tide of frustration stymies your progress, and the powerful waves of life's challenges crash against your midship you will not lose your position and drift away aimlessly. You will remain steadfast and stable. The strongest anchor you can utilize as you build your business is knowing your Why. In other words, the deep-seated reason(s) why you're not only going to do this, but committed to seeing it through. An individual's Why is the greatest and strongest anchor known to man. When you know your why and have committed it to be your driving purpose then you become unshakable and immovable in your convictions. There is no one and nothing that will tear you away from what you are fighting and striving for. Finding your anchor and then dropping it has to be the most important task that you begin with on your journey to building an extraordinary business and extraordinary life. If you ask any leader in your current opportunity or business if they have their anchor in place, they will give you resounding "yes" and probably recite it without a moment's notice if asked to. There are others that even carry around their reason(s) written on a piece of paper. For so many of us, however, our Whys are written on the tablets of our hearts. Genuine business giants, seasoned veterans, and those that have weathered the storms will tell you that their anchors are securely in place. The challenge that I have found, after being in the people business for more than half my life, is that the majority of people do not take this part of growing their business seriously. Somehow, they feel that the notion of knowing, writing down and committing to your true motive and basis is hokey. It is an aspect of their initial business development that they find very little value in allocating time to do. This is the biggest blunder any success-seeking entrepreneur can make. It is a surefire way to not surviving your first year or so in this business. When everything else gets ugly, your Why has to be the most attractive thing left.

I can recall when I decided to become an entrepreneur and build my own business that my "Why" early on was not the reason I have now, to a certain degree. By the way, that is ok too. Your Why is subject to change over time. In fact, there is a part of it that should evolve and mature as you and your business does. The grounds for your anchor now may not be what they are one year from now. Incidentally, this is a good thing because it shows that you are growing in your understanding of the potential that your business can deliver. When I first started, my Why was simply to make it work because I did not want my colleagues and business partners to look at me like a loser because I quit. These people were a heck of a lot sharper than me and I didn't want them to think that I did not belong. Besides that, my concern was that I would miss the opportunity if it turned out that the leaders of that company were right. I had always disliked the idea of missing out or being left out and if that opportunity was going to deliver then I wanted in. If this was going to become a winning team, then I wanted to be a part of it. My motivation, at that time and age, was not to be financially free or have luxury or anything like that. I resolved that if my business efforts yielded an extra $1,500 a month that would be fine as well. My anchor was shaped by pride, self respect, and fear of loss. I knew that no matter what, this dude was going to make it work, no matter how hard it got. Whatever was needed to be learned, I would learn it. I had dropped the anchor. As it turns out, my Whys have changed a number of times over the years but they have still provided the anchoring when needed. The truth is that if these anchors had been missing from my business life then I would probably have quit a long time ago. I am thankful that I had them and still continue to until this day. You need anchors, my friends. If at the reading of this book you still have not taken the time to search your heart and mind for the reasons why you want to succeed in your business then stop right now and in the few spaces below begin to jot down your Why. That's right, right now. If you know them already then quickly jot them down as a reminder. However, if you have never given this thought and you are under the impression that you will build a big business without first knowing your Why then you are kidding yourself.

Therefore, stop everything and take the next few minutes to dig deep and do a little soul searching and find your Why. Locate the anchor. Write it down. Don't worry if it is not a complete thought or a bit sketchy, you can always come back to clarify and modify it later. The key is to get started. Do it now. If you don't take the time now then another excuse will get in the way. Go ahead and use the lines below. When you do, trust me, you will begin to feel empowered and even emotionally connected with your opportunity. It will take on a new perspective. So go ahead. I'll wait.

_____

_____

_____

_____

_____

_____

Believe me, unless you did this brief, yet essential assignment the rest of this book will be meaningless and ineffective in helping you survive. You may limp along in your business for a while but long term you will not make it. I have seen too many great people whither during a stretch of difficult times and never recover. Inasmuch, I have seen some of the greatest and inspiring examples of fortitude during turbulent times because those individuals had their Why committed to memory and imbedded in their hearts. It is amazing to see what anchored people can sustain and weather when the high tides of frustration and windstorms of disappointment begin to toss their ship like a toddler toy. Find your Why. Otherwise, what's going to keep you from quitting when you fail the licensing exam more than once; when you still struggle with skill development six months later; when no one shows up to your presentations or one on one appointments; when your own friends and family won't return your calls or don't become clients; when the commission you receive turns out to be a lot less than what you were expecting; when your colleagues or co-workers bad mouth your company and the opportunity? Heck, some of you can add your own example right here too. The point is that survival in your business early on will depend on how well you stand up to the inevitable and inescapable trials that every entrepreneur faces. No one is absolved of them. Yet, nothing else will help you remain resolute and unswerving than determining your Why and then dropping the anchor.

## *How can I apply this Chapter to my business?*

_____

_____

_____

_____

_____

_____

_____

_____

_____

_____

_____

_____

_____

_____

_____

_____

_____

# CHAPTER 2

*"The only way to get anywhere is to start from where you are."*

William Lee

## "DON'T FORGET YOUR STORY"

The most powerful marketing tool you have is your personal story. We all have one. Now, you might be thinking, "what story?" Or "I don't have a story." I hear this often. Well, the truth is that you do have a story. Your story is why you are so passionate about your business, how you got involved, what motivated you to make a decision to join your company, what your expectations are, and how you see this business making an impact on people and your family. This is your story.

It is the story that connects the dots for your prospect as to why you do what you do. It is what melts the barriers between salesman and client, recruiter and prospect, mentor and apprentice. Yet I find that it is the least used resource that new associates utilize in growing their business in the early stages. In fact, it's almost as if they shy away from telling it. My summation has been that they feel awkward in sharing their heartfelt personal account and that no one would really care to hear it anyway. This is a big mistake. Everyone has a few specific reasons why they decided to get involved in business. What motivated them to step out in faith and venture in uncomfortable and uncharted territory and it needs to be shared. It is what makes your presentation come alive and involving. My experience has taught me that people are not interested in what you have to offer inasmuch as they are intrigued with the story behind the person making the offer. Your story is what makes you genuine and relatable to people who are looking for someone to relate to. Whether you are recruiting a prospect or creating a client out of one, the overlapping approach is the same. Starting with the genesis of your involvement creates honesty and transparency that soon develops into the trust that is ever so critical if someone will ever do business with you, join your business, or refer you to others.

I have been telling mine for the last twenty years. My story has only gotten better over time mainly for two reasons; anything that you say repeatedly over time will get better the more you say it, but my experiences along the way have served to add dimension to it. It has become more relatable to a broader audience and has harbored greater appeal to the masses. Yet, this did not happen overnight nor was my story super fancy when I first started. My story was basic, straightforward, funny, yet appealing. If I may, I'd like to share it with you.

My decision to get started in this business resulted from a first hand experience on how lack of financial education affected my family so I purposed in my heart to never have my future family struggle the way we did growing up. My parents came from Puerto Rico in the early 1960's and settled in the Spanish Harlem section of Manhattan. While they lacked academic wisdom they were not short on common sense. They were hard workers and understood the value of saving yet were never taught the principles or strategies like those who have money are taught. It seemed that the financial institutions were more concerned or geared to attracting those who had the financial means to make it worthwhile for them. So, naturally my parents would not have qualified for the attention or effort of any financial services person whatsoever. I saw this as unfair and unjust but that was the system. Then one day, one of my personal training clients (and friend now) invited me to see a presentation, so we met at his office and left together. He was a real estate broker, so I didn't question where we were going because I figured it had to do with real estate. Now at that time, the 1992 Presidential Elections had just been held and presidential candidate Ross Perot had been very popular. My client happened to be playing a tape of a guy that sounded a lot like Ross Perot so I thought we were going to see him at some real estate meeting. I later found out that it was a recording of Art Williams (the founder of A. L. Williams). As such, I sat through a presentation that changed my life. Even though I could not figure out how "mutual fun" was going to help anybody with investing (they were actually talking about a *mutual fund*), but I knew that the financial education I was about to receive would change my family's future forever. In the end, my decision to join was based on the fact that I had nothing to lose and everything to gain, both financially and personally. It was clear to me that I needed financial education and so did many of my friends, family, and colleagues. Yet, notwithstanding them, I knew that there was a large segment of the population that had never been exposed to the concepts that I learned in just the last 20 minutes. Besides that, my academic career would have never demanded a six figure income with a fancy downtown corner office but instead a six dollar happy meal in a six story apartment building. It did not take me long to realize that I could make good money by helping people learn about money. Momma didn't raise no fool! I decided to join and give it a try. Has my decision paid off? A resounding yes! Over my career, my decision to do this has positively impacted thousands of people who have received the financial education and information that has created a better financial experience for them and their family. Today, even though the company I represent is different from its predecessor, I am still as thrilled to help people today as I was back then. I consider it an honor and privilege to do that. Nice. Relatable. Heartfelt story. Wouldn't you agree?

One final note. Be yourself and tell your story and not somebody else's. Don't compare yours with that of another and feel you have to alter it to make it appealing. Be authentic. Your personal account does not have to be funny, sad, or even exciting. In fact, it may even be downright uneventful, but who cares? It is your story. None of these are a prerequisite to how effective your story will be anyway. One thing to remember, however, is that you are sharing a brief personal story not giving an oral documentary of your ancestry. No one is interested in that. So go ahead and share it knowing that everyone loves the story of the humble go-getter who has a sincere desire to achieve life-changing greatness through hard work. If for no other reason, you'll garner the support from those individuals just because they'll respect, admire, or flat out love your story.

# *How can I apply this Chapter to my business?*

_____

_____

_____

_____

_____

_____

_____

_____

_____

_____

_____

_____

_____

_____

_____

_____

# CHAPTER 3

*"To accept good advice is but to increase one's own ability."*

Johann Wolfgang von Goethe

## "MILK YOUR MENTOR"

Abuse them or lose them. In every successful business you'll find those mentors that are willing to spend as much time as needed in developing their people. These company superstars are the business giants that all new associates want to emulate and model their business and success after. It is almost without question that these entrepreneurial legends have mastered the skill sets and can provide an enormous volume of personal experience and insight, not to mention, the basic "how to's" in abundance. Sadly, not enough new associates and business novices abuse their mentor's time, energy, and expertise. By foregoing the open door policy that mentors make readily available to new colleagues, they prolong their success and the inevitable learning curve that comes with every new enterprise and skill set. Take advantage of that mentor who is willing to pour into you his time and nuggets of wisdom. Milk them for all they've got. I can promise you that they won't mind just as long as you bear the fruit of that invaluable experience and coaching. However, I would be remiss if I didn't take a moment to state that your mentor is also a business person who is building his business for himself and his family as well. Therefore, he or she is not a door mat, a psychologist, a psychiatrist, a marriage counselor, or a child therapist. There is not a business mentor, teacher, pastor, coach, etc. that will allow his time, energy, and at times, money to be taken advantage of by someone who does not take their advice to heart and begin applying it. Your mentor will only make himself available to those who are genuinely serious about success. As a mentor to many, I can tell you that I only focus my efforts on those that show, by their actions, not words, that they mean business. Some time ago, as our team was growing and prospering, I was asked by a new associate how I was able to determine whom to spend my time on when there were so many. And who I would allow to milk me for my time and focus? I recall my answer to him clearly today as if it were yesterday because I still practice the same discipline. I said to him, "Well, the winners, of course". That only led him to ask, with an even more perplexed look on his face, "How do you know who the winners are when when they are so new to the business? I mean, they don't have a winner sign posted on their forehead, you know." I replied that he was right and that there was no way to tell who the winners were that I was going to devote more time to that early on, with one exception. The exception is (and always will be) obvious. The winners always show up. They show up to every event, every meeting, and every training. They show up early when asked to and stay late without being asked to. They even show up when they are told not to show up. They somehow find a way to get in. They are on every conference call. They read every book suggested. They bring a notebook and recorder to training. They take action not orders. The winners exhibit behaviors that are outside the norm of the average new associate. This is how I identified some being worth the while of pouring special time and interest into. This was (and again, still is) the kind of new individual who, as a leader of many, I will give special attention when asked to. I can speak with almost certainty that many other mentors and leaders would agree with this wholeheartedly. Personally, I don't have any issues with this type of new associate milking me as their mentor because the early indication dictates that my efforts will be met with a great return. The very important lesson here is that you should aggressively pursue the attention and time of your mentor but you must first display to them that you are worth the investment of their time. Your mentor will gladly and willingly allow you to milk him for his invaluable talents, training, skills, special recruiting or sales phone calls, meetings, whatever, just as long as you show initiative and not take anything for granted.

I have experienced the value of milking my mentors in my prior company and current one also. My current mentor often claims that if he had more teammates that were on his butt like I am that he would never get anything done. By the very nature of his statement, I can tell that not enough of his business partners seek him for advice, coaching, and experience. That is a total shame. I have always been keenly aware of how this business model works so I have never bypassed the opportunity to professionally abuse my mentor. As a result, we both have experienced greater success and a great friendship to boot. He would tell you himself that he would not trade the times that he has helped me, on many levels, grow my business. Now, you might be asking why any mentor would want to have his precious time and energy monopolized by a few. Why would my mentor do these things for me? For that answer to really sink in, you need to understand the stroke of genius in our compensation model. The greatest feature of our industry's compensation model is that, simply put, when you get paid, your mentor gets paid. If you make a bunch of money then he or she makes a bunch of money. If you make it fast, he or she makes it fast. If you make it slow, he or she makes it slow. If you make no money, then they'll make no money, at least not from your efforts. So, you quickly have to draw the conclusion that your mentor has an absolute financial interest in your success. So, it behooves him or her to provide exclusive mentorship to those new associates who display the most promise. Your mentor has incentives to do so. This awesome dynamic is hardly found in most corporate job settings at all. In most job scenarios, the manager, owner, or president stands to gain financially whether or not you are mentored by him. In fact, it's rare that any manager will spend more time than he is paid for to expend any more of his energy, talents, and experience than necessary. True? He will only provide just enough so that he doesn't lose his job but not enough for you to potentially cost him his or a promotion. As far as owners or presidents, the average person never gets close enough for the owner or president to know their name, let alone, mentor them. It's an almost ridiculous thought. These individuals have absolutely no incentive to because they will still get paid no matter what you do or don't do. It is why I say to you, right now, take advantage of the fact that you are in a business system where you do have a successful mentor that is willing to help you and teach you success principles. Nowhere in America does such a system exist where it costs you nothing to milk your mentor. These success principles will help you avoid the business pitfalls while aiding you in arriving at your desired destination faster, smarter, and well prepared for the next level.

## How can I apply this Chapter to my business?

_____

_____

_____

_____

_____

_____

_____

_____

_____

_____

_____

_____

_____

_____

_____

_____

# CHAPTER 4

*"The difference between mediocrity and greatness is extra effort."*

George Allen

## "MASTER THE WORDS"

If a picture paints a thousand words then a word or phrase can equally elicit a thousand emotions, and since we are emotionally-driven beings, this is a skill development that cannot be overlooked, taken lightly, or shortchanged. In the people business, effective communication is everything and a bag of chips. The right word can draw someone closer to you and sympathize with your cause or they can repel and drive that individual away. Now, I am not proposing that unless you are a gifted orator or a wordsmith you cannot win big in your business but there has to be a mastery of some key words and phrases. Hopefully, in your particular business there should be a set of scripts, word coaching, or a mentor that you can copy which can help you develop the proper terminology to be an effective recruiter or salesperson in your business. There are many who fail miserably quite early in their business simply because they forego this area of skill development. As a result, frustration sets in when they cannot seem to attract anyone to, at the very least, hear them out. Understanding that human beings are designed to react emotionally and then rationally, your communication and the words you use must appeal to the heart and not the head. The right phrases, words, and (in the advanced stage) questions can lead your prospect to draw upon positive or negative experiences which can play a significant role in what they decide to do. Having a fundamental knowledge of "good words" or "bad words" and how to use them is imperative in developing the confidence needed to survive.

I find often that a new associate's biggest struggle is not knowing what to say. This becomes the crux of their business growth and what can lead so many to quit. Over the years, as I have spoken to many other leaders from many different companies, we have all agreed that if there was one thing that holds most new associates back from exploding their business with a record setting fast start is not being comfortable in communicating with prospects. Somehow, I sense that as you are reading this you agree as well. You have also found yourself in a quagmire. You believe in your heart that your company is great. You are convinced of the goodness of the product or service you offer. Clearly, the marketplace is in need of it. Lack of desire and ambition is not the concern here either. Yet, you can't seem to open your mouth and talk to people. The most important part of your business is talking to people and yet, you have a big "CLOSED" sign on the front door. Ultimately, I don't believe it is totally fear of rejection that is the root of the problem but lack of confidence. This confidence is bred when there is the sense that you can get a result. If you knew that for every prospect you spoke to you would get a desired result then you would have no problem in talking to more people. Well, having a working knowledge of the effective words that have proven successful for others should be of your utmost aggressive pursuit. This is why it is priority to seek the scripts that your company offers. Study the leaders in your business and copy what they say. Pick up the resources available that will develop your usage of words. Have fun role playing with your colleagues your new prospecting vernacular. Practice, drill, and rehearse until it becomes second nature to you. This is how you win big in your business and become a legend. There are associates and leaders, not only from my business but from others as well, who often ask me to how did I get so good or why does it seem so natural when I am prospecting? My answer is that I have mastered the words. I know the proper words for the proper person in the proper setting. It is rare that I am caught off guard. My wife tells me all the time that she is amazed at how I can go from one subject of conversation with someone and then in an instant totally switch gears, seamlessly, and dive into the word zone with a new prospect. It's the reason she won't take me with her when she shops. She knows I will stop and talk to EVERYONE. Well, the reason for this is that I am constantly working on my words, phrases, and questions. My mind and vocal cords are synchronized with each other and programmed with impactful and effective terminology. It was important for me to learn them early on and I stopped at nothing until I got better and better. Your survival is largely dependent on how fast you learn the words.

Before we go any further let me give you anxious folks a reason for a sigh of relief. There will be times that regardless whatever words or phrases you use the recipient will not react in the manner that you would have liked or anticipated.

This is simply because they were not ready to receive your message at the moment in time you delivered it. It happens. It has nothing to do with you. It has everything to do with them. You can't say the wrong thing to the right person inasmuch as you can't say the right thing to the wrong person. Timing plays just as much of an important part as does the words you use. I have experienced this myself many times in the last twenty years. While wanting everyone I prospected or approached to take favorable action (a healthy perspective for any business builder), I have encountered that even the most appealing usage of words did not get me the results I was hoping for. It was just that the individual I was talking with was not ready to receive my offer or grant my appeal. It happens. The key is to continue working on your word library. Decide that you will commit a few key words and phrases to memory and then practice new phrases daily and your confidence will grow. Incidentally, your confidence will reach new levels when you finally realize how simple it is and will continue to be. It amazes me when a new colleague attempts to re-invent the wheel by coming up with his own, untested, unproven scripts or wordplay and falls flat on their face when the results are minimal, if any at all. Don't make your first twelve months in this business harder than it needs to be. If you throw your ingenuity into idle for a little while, check the pride baggage at the door, and delete the blueprint of whatever you think you know and embrace a humble approach to learning and developing this area, then you will have fun prospecting and filling up your calendar with activity.

Over the years I have taught my own teammates as well as outsiders a few simple yet positive and effective words/phrases as well as words/phrases to stay away from because they draw negative connotations, emotions, and imagery. The use of negative words/phrases can quickly squelch any budding interest that a prospect might have been stirring up. On the other hand, positive words and phrases (which I call glamour words) can stoke the fire of interest by calling upon the power of fascination. The way you use these simple words or phrases in a sentence will determine how quickly you ascend in your business stardom. Many of my business colleagues have seen their activity levels dramatically increase due to exchanging their old word habits with new ones. I'd like to share some of the Glamour Words and Negative Words I'm speaking of along with better alternatives. Obviously, there many more than these provided and your company or leaders have their own as well. However, the point is to start developing the skill and applying it immediately.

## *Glamour Words (Phrases)*

Glamour words can elicit a positive and bigger picture because they are words that are rich in-depth and perception. The more you masterfully use these words the more impressed your prospect will be with not only your conversational skills but they will feel extremely confident that they can, one day, introduce their prospect to you.

*Community of like-minded professionals*
*Business Partner*
*Colleague*
*Prestigious*
*Enterprising abilities*
*Skilled professionals*
*Ambassador of Good Will*

*Agents of Influence*
*Corporate Overview*
*Corporate Briefing*
*Better investment experience*
*Specialists in retirement repair*
*A get together to highlight some of our leading ideas*
*A unique business model*
*We're different by design*
*Examine our enterprise*
*A snapshot of our in demand resources*
*A global company with a grassroots approach*
*Performance-based compensation package*
*Company initiatives*

## <u>Negative Words</u>

The following words have been so overused that they surface memories of unpleasant experiences. They conjure up too many awkward and uncomfortable emotions.

**Opportunity** *(every one and their mother has an opportunity these days)*

**Meeting** *(nobody wants to attend another meeting)*

**Sales** *(nobody wants to buy and nobody wants to sell <u>anything</u>)*

**Manager** *(this is another word for "oppressive person telling me what to do")*

**Upline** *(sounds network marketing/multi-level "ish")*

**Downline** *(we won't even go there on this one)*

**Teammate** (most people don't comprehend the concept)

**Appointment** (many people equate this word with pain or discomfort)

**Cost** (need I say more?)

**Join** (nobody wants to join anything because it screams of another time or money commitment that they have to make; besides this, cults are started by people who "join")

## Instead of negative words use positive words or phrases

**Opportunity**—What we offer; our unique business model; a platform of programs that help people

**Meeting**—A corporate briefing, a get together to highlight some of our leading ideas, career open house

**Sales**—Providing a service; fulfilling a need; making an impact; agents of influence

**Manager**—colleague; business partner; mentor; the individual I work closely with

**Upline**—mentor; business coach

**Downline/Teammates**—colleagues, group of like-minded professionals, skilled professionals, business partners, fraternity of entrepreneurs

**Appointment**—pop by; drop by; catch up with you to simply summarize our ideas

**Cost**—fee for service; initial investment; your deductible expense;

***Join***—build an alliance together; a privilege to be in business with you; get involved

Now, to help you comprehend with greater clarity and exhortation why this is so important, I believe that a hands-on illustration is suitable. I'll provide for you two brief versions of an invitation by a new associate to a prospect. One version is flat out, "throw up" awful and the other is . . . well, you be the judge.

## ***Version One***

"Hey, Joe. How's it going? Good! Listen, I was wondering if you could come with me to check out this business opportunity tomorrow night. The meeting starts at 7. By the way, I'll introduce you to my manager. He's the best upline in the business. Also, if you like what you see then you can join under me and be a part of my downline. It only costs a $100 to join, if you decide to. Anyway, can you make it?"

Now, I know what some of you are thinking. Some of you are thinking, "Wow. That sounded pretty good. What's wrong with that?" For those of you that are actually thinking this, please email me your name and I will pray for you. The others are thinking, "No way. Who would ever say that to anyone? It's crazy." Well, you'd be surprised. In fact, the cold hard reality is that a lot of you have already said stuff that sounds a lot like (if not darn near identical to) version one. And, you wonder why nobody says "yes" to your offer or request.

## *Version Two*

"Hey, Joe. How's it going? Good! Listen, I need to ask you a favor. There is a global company that I have been researching recently that shares the same passions and concerns that I have regarding helping people. I've been impressed with their grassroots approach. I know the firm is conducting a briefing tomorrow evening to discuss their expansion plans and since you have a knack for enterprise, would you mind accompanying me and giving me your honest assessment? If nothing else, you can become my ambassador of good will as I move forward with the company. Would you do me that favor?"

Do you see the difference? Which version would have appealed to you if I had approached you in this way? Without a shadow of a doubt, version two. Oh, there are so many more examples like these, my friends. In fact, a whole other handbook can be written just on this very critical survival topic alone. My final point is for you not to disregard the importance of mastering words. There is no substitute for the confidence you can develop because you have committed to your mental and verbal library the verbiage necessary to ensure that your calendar is full of activity. Embrace this skill and you'll see that your chances for survival have just become even greater.

## *How can I apply this Chapter to my business?*

_____

_____

_____

_____

_____

_____

_____

_____

_____

_____

_____

_____

_____

_____

_____

_____

_____

# CHAPTER 5

*"If you can't fly, then run. If you can't run, then walk. If you can't walk, then crawl. But whatever you do, keep moving."*

Martin Luther King, Jr.

## "SEEK OUT THE RESOURCES"

If your intent is to survive the initial phase of your business then becoming very familiar with the company resources available to aid you through this phase should be your daily mission. The fact is, most businesses provide their new associates enough resources to become well equipped, competent, and confident in their new opportunity. The challenge is that most new associates never use them. With technology as vast (and growing) as it is today, there is no shortage of mediums provided by your company to help you win big and grow a dynamic and thriving business by being properly trained. The tools that are created for the new entrepreneur in your business are better than they have ever been. Yet, it seems that the more it becomes available the less they are sought out by new associates.

This is a major error to commit especially in the all too precious early stages of your business development and survival. Embracing a "sponge-like attitude" is the answer. Whatever the company has made available is designed and usually proven to be effective in helping you get through the natural learning curve as efficiently and smoothly as possible. These resources are designed to increase your level of understanding, competence, and thereby, confidence.

Frequently, in the early stages of your business one of the stumbling blocks that you will encounter is having the desire to share with others your business but falling short at either starting that process or feeling awkward or incompetent once you've begun. This is usually due to not having a decent grip on what makes your opportunity special or unique. Not surprisingly, you can't effectively give what you don't have. The ineptness you feel is due to the lack of understanding or shortage of information which results from the meager attempts at seeking the resources. Consider how far the most expensive, pimped up, high tech car will go with an empty gas tank? Not very far. Well, neither will you unless you gas up by using the tools available. It never ceases to amaze me when I get questions asked or concerns raised by new associates about topics, systems, products, etc. of which the answers are readily available via the company site, company manual, or a simple phone call to the home office. This immediately tells me that my new associate is not spending any time in familiarizing themselves with the company information they have access to. However, limiting yourself just to the resources that are only provided by your company will serve to slow your learning curve, your business development, and thereby, your cash flow. The bottom line is that you are the one that is ultimately responsible for your business growth and the heights it can reach. There is no one that will spoon feed you what you need to know to become successful. The blame falls squarely on you if you fail to achieve success because of your lack of aggressiveness in seeking the resources. You will not survive if you do. There are inevitable pitfalls and mistakes that accompany any new endeavor and are a natural part of growing a business. There will be plenty of the "do over moments" when you wish you could have the moment back to re-do because you would have said or done something differently. Yet, the ability to recover and learn from your mistakes will be determined by how well you were prepared for them in the first place. The degree and severity of the mistake or mishap will only be mild if you equip yourself sufficiently through the use of whatever training tools are at your disposal.

Now, you may be asking "What are some of the more important resources that I should be seeking then? With so much available, what's priority?" These are great questions because it is easy for an excited new associate to become overwhelmed and inundated with so many of the resources available that paralysis of analysis sets in. This is the other side of the coin and presents a viable conundrum because there should be a sincere and aggressive pursuit of knowledge but not to the extreme where you do nothing else. That doesn't work either. I have seen new associates go to either extreme and the result, usually, is a very slow moving start, if any at all, or death by information brain freeze. There has to be a balance of knowledge acquisition and resource research with action and execution. Without a balanced approach, your days are numbered. It really only becomes a matter of time before you "fold em' and walk away". So, what are the most important resources to seek?

The resources that will teach you how to communicate your opportunity effectively. Period. The modules that confidently equip you at telling your company story, the goodness of the product or services you offer, and the compensation plan are all integral parts of communicating your opportunity to another person. In my business, there are licensing requirements. Therefore, the resources to become licensed quickly so that one can get paid are priority. If your opportunity requires similar licensing or credentials in order to receive compensation, then that is a priority. Please keep in mind, however, that resources are not limited to just books, webinars, or online materials but can take the shape of conversations, weekly office training, quarterly big events, or one on one training with your manager. It can mean that you interview one of the top performers or leaders in your office or in someone else's office. Early on, when I wanted to get really good at recruiting top financial professionals (which requires a very different approach and skill set) I sought the resource of my mentor and recorded him while he made recruiting calls to top notch industry people. I took notes as I heard him masterfully entice and fascinate these individuals. It was only a matter of time before I was making the same calls with the same level of success as he was having. Today, I am his number one recruiter generally but, by far, of industry professionals. Those phone calls that I recorded and heard numerous times over have become one of the most important and prized resources that I have ever sought.

I'd like to add one last point to this subject. If you can't find the information that you need within your company's sphere of resources, or if additional is needed, then don't hesitate to go outside of your circle or comfort zone to find what you need to win. If you need help in one particular area or another then don't stop searching or seeking until you find the material that will help you get through survival that much quicker. You have no excuse in this department. Personal growth, which invariably leads to business growth, must be intentional and disciplined. You have to schedule time for it. Lastly, whether you are a Believer as I am or not, there is a great lesson taught by Jesus in the Bible that is totally applicable here. He says in Matthew 7:7, "Ask, and it will be given to you; seek, and you will find; knock, and it will be opened to you." Truer words were never spoken.

## How can I apply this Chapter to my business?

_____

_____

_____

_____

_____

_____

_____

_____

_____

_____

_____

_____

_____

_____

_____

_____

# CHAPTER 6

*"Take time to deliberate, but when the time for action arrives, stop thinking and go in."*
Andrew Jackson

## "KNOW THE LAW"

**W**ould you ever consider brushing your teeth once or twice a week? If you did, then before you'd know it your teeth would decay, become brittle, ineffective and eventually even fall out. This would have consequences on the whole digestive process. You would still survive but the whole process would not be as pleasant because the aspect of the assembly line that starts everything off right is missing . . . your teeth. The inconsistency in the daily care and brushing of them would cause the whole system to run poorly. Well, comparably, if you would never entertain for a second practicing oral hygiene on a once or twice a week basis because of the inescapable consequences, then why would you treat prospecting any different? Hence, prospecting and talking to people has to be as consistent and daily as brushing your teeth. This is what the unwritten law in our industry calls attention to. You will not find this unwritten law on any company brochure or on the homepage of any company website. The marketing material does not cover it. Yet, there are violators in droves. In fact, so many commit this violation so often that they never recover from the penalty. The eventual insurmountable penalty is unrecoverable discouragement and disappointment, and soon thereafter, the exiting of their business opportunity. This law is the Law of Large Numbers. It constitutes that operating a high numbers or a high people contact discipline will catapult your business and hence, your goals and dreams to the desired end result. It is that simple and straightforward. This is a fundamental that you must begin to execute vigorously and daily. If your business or career thrives on your story being shared with large numbers of people then you cannot afford to consistently violate this law. It will cost you dearly. Incidentally, by not obeying the Law of Large Numbers you are, by default, exercising the Law of Small Numbers. The Law of Small Numbers states that in an opportunity or environment that requires a massive dissemination of information daily, you decide to cherry pick who you will talk to. The Law of Small Numbers goes on to state that you take it upon yourself to be the judge and jury of who deserves to have an offer made to them. Or worse, you take it upon yourself to determine who would not be interested. This Law further asserts that your approach to making contacts or prospecting new people is not focused, lacks daily order, and is extremely nonchalant. The ongoing practice of this Law will destroy any potential that you could have had. It leads to the inevitable death of your possibilities of winning. Consider this: the only people that will never join your business or become clients are the ones you never talk to. I believe that one of the earliest examples of the incredible power of the Law of Large Numbers can be found in the Bible. Now, I know what some of you are thinking, "Now that's a stretch, Jay." Well, hang in there with me and you'll see.

In the Old Testament, when God told Abraham to be fruitful and multiply, He understood the Law of Large Numbers. God understood that in order for Him to get his expansion plan off the ground it was going to take a lot of people. A whole lot of people. It is one of the early examples we have of the Law of Large Numbers at work. Unfortunately, not enough industry entrepreneurs seem to gravitate to this way of thinking or get stuck somewhere in the middle. As a result, their businesses never really take off because they applied small numbers to a large numbers equation. In other words, they fail to realize that a set number of people are almost programmed to say "no", "not now", "maybe", etc., but so are a set number of people who are open to saying "yes". Jim Rohn once said "There really are only a few negative people in the whole world that do not have in interest in anything whatsoever. The problem is that they move around a lot". Hence, the Law of Large Numbers dictates that as your numbers increase so will your "no" encounters but equally so will your "yes" encounters. Some universal laws will never change no matter what the theme. They are applicable to every scenario. Bear in mind, the farmer who is desirous of a bountiful harvest would never consider sowing just a handful of seeds and then truly believe that his harvest will come from those few chosen seeds. He comprehends that the more seed he sows, the more the reality of his expectations will come to pass. Well, the business or career that you have chosen has the same attributes. The more seeds you sow, the more harvest you will reap. Now, here is the fun part of it all; it's predictable. In other words, the outcome is predictable when you begin to apply the Law of Large Numbers to your business efforts. There is a non-debatable fact of the Law of Large Numbers. Ready? Quantity yields quality. Or, as I have always said, "many duds bring a few studs." There is no other way around it. I wish there was but every successful leader in every business opportunity or sales business will concur that this is the way it works. You will not change this dynamic unless you get your own planet one day and rearrange the rules.

Let's just take this one step further for even greater clarification and really drive the point home for some of you thick-headed folks. If the previously mentioned farmer decided to go against the Law and hand pick a small number of seeds (the real pretty ones that looked like they had so much potential, in his opinion) and plant them, then go back home and wait for the harvest in a few months, what do you think he will see come harvest time? Right! He will see himself starving to death. Why? Because those seeds that he thought would do something did not. Those lazy ol', good for nuthin' seeds produced zero harvest! Would you say that the poor old farmer lost his farming mojo? Probably not, but he lost his mind if he thought that a few seeds would do the job of providing a grand harvest. What he did not realize is that Murphy's Law throws its two cents into it and says that he was just a few seeds short of a bountiful harvest, if only he had planted a few more. Do you get the picture yet? One final point: The Law of Large Numbers will always produce some that will and some that won't. That is a variable that not you, nor I, nor anybody else will ever control. The sooner you know and accept the Law, the closer you will be to surviving.

## *How can I apply this Chapter to my business?*

_____

_____

_____

_____

_____

_____

_____

_____

_____

_____

_____

_____

_____

_____

_____

_____

# CHAPTER 7

*"Nothing can stop the man with the right mental attitude from achieving his goal; nothing on earth can help the man with the wrong mental attitude."*

Thomas Jefferson

## "EMPLOYEE VERSUS EMPLOYER MINDSET"

Old habits can be hard to break. The habit of employee thinking is one such example. Now of course I recognize that there are a good number of people that will read this book who are currently or previously owners of their own business, sales professionals, or managers. Therefore, a lot of what you will read about in this chapter may be what you practice already or certainly believe. If this is your case, then I encourage you to use this book as a way to re-emphasize this principle to your new colleagues or team members. The habit of thinking like an employee is a habit that will absolutely destroy your business if not addressed immediately. The challenge, naturally, is for those that are currently working as an employee to be able to delineate both patterns of thought and separate them at the appropriate times. Now, that being said, it will take a disciplined effort that is put forth daily and consistently. If not, you will succumb to the employee mentality syndrome again. Yes, the battle will be daily. The Bible says that oil and water do not mix. They have nothing in common. Such is the case with an employee and an employer mentality. They do not have anything in common. Not even close. They are worlds apart. So, your challenge will be to slowly develop the employer mentality and the habits, disciplines, attitudes, and thoughts that accompany that way of thinking. As you will discover, this new mindset and attributes are totally contrary to that of the employee mindset. Sadly, many new independent business owners are never quite able to make the transition and find that their business life is short lived or shortchanged. At the height of the employee to employer mindset transition is the comprehension that an employee processes activity or a predetermined set of instructions while an employer creates it. An employee is a work processor while an employer is a work creator. The longer the employee has been in that setting the longer the mental wiring has had opportunity to weld. Hence, the harder it can be to reconfigure the wiring and, naturally, new thinking and action habits. To the degree that you embrace and effectively transition from employee mentality to employer mentality will determine the degree of how quickly you graduate from survival to thriving.

If there is one that thing that has to go by the wayside if you are to have a triumphant conversion from work processor to work creator as an independent business professional or owner is the old habits of an employee. Not that the habits are bad habits (some of them are very good and will serve you well in your business) but they have been configured for a different a purpose. Namely, a job. These habits have been implemented to assist someone else's work formation and projects. Therefore, they don't necessarily apply here. For example, generally in most employment situations your schedule is fixed with set hours of work. You know that you will start at a certain time, break for lunch at a predictably set time, and end your work day also at a routine time. This type of daily routine is very banal, predictable, and comfortable because there are, by and large, no surprises. Your conventional day provides very little for what you are not prepared for. As a result, it is a relatively safe and stable employee experience that is easy to get accustomed to. You may not necessarily like what you do, or like your fellow co-workers, or your boss but it is familiar grounds. Well, this lifestyle or mindset could not be further from that of an employer or a business entrepreneur. Typically, there is nothing routine about an employer. Although, there are a set amount of activities that are planned daily, the execution of those activities and the whole day, for that matter, is anything but predictable, safe, and stable. Whether you are an employer, or budding new business entrepreneur, or anyone in an independent sales driven profession, there is nothing truly fixed or commonplace. To survive past your early juncture in this business you must understand that your schedule will have nothing preset about it. Don't look for the similar patterns of a work schedule because you won't find it. There is no one to tell you when to come in to the office, what time to start working or what time you have to stay until. Your time is truly your own and no one is monitoring it. You, not someone else, design your own schedule. Yes, you have freedom but with that freedom comes responsibility. No one is going to hand you activity to process; you will have to create it. I have found that many of my prior business partners were never able to turn the switch from employee to employer thinking and therefore never developed the mindset and the disciplines to endure past the initial learning curve of their business. I recall one time early in my career when a very enthusiastic individual joined our business and got off to a great start. I was very excited about him because of his tenacity and workhorse approach to building his business. There was never a meeting that he would miss and always brought new guests with him. After a few weeks, he had about 10 solid individuals on his team that were consistent with attendance and were even in the licensing phase. Interestingly enough, one day he pulls me to the side and begins to share with me that his people were getting somewhat discouraged. When I asked him why, he began to tell me that they were wondering when they were going to get paid. After all, he continued, they have been showing up, attending calls, and in licensing class but weren't as of yet generating an income. He further added that it was not right that they were doing so much work and not making any money. Now, I can honestly tell you that I had to take my shoe off, as well as my socks, in order to get my jaw and place it back on my face. There was no way, I thought to myself, that this dude was serious. However, he was dead serious and so were his teammates. At that moment, I realized that even though they knew that this was their own business and not a job, per se, that the employee mental wiring was overpowering the ongoing message that was drilled often in training. Somehow, they equated that their "work efforts" deserved to be compensated. It goes without saying that they did not survive very long. As funny or outlandish as this may sound, some of you reading this book have already had that same, ingrained wiring vying for your attention and causing havoc in your thought patterns. This employee mentality wiring is triggering messages that are uttering to you, "You keep attending those meetings, buying those products, studying for licensing, making phone calls, going on appointments, Saturday mornings sessions, spending time and money on gas, travel, business cards, and marketing, attending webinars, making invitations and what have you got to show for it? Where's the money after doing all of this?" This subtle, mental debate will be your greatest enemy in your fight to survive your first year.

In my opinion, there are great benefits and privileges in developing an employer mindset that by far outweigh not developing one. First, you get to determine who you want to work with and be in business with. Think about that for a second. As an employee, would that typically be possible? Nope. How incredible and liberating is the idea that you can go into business with people you enjoy, share same passions, are like-minded, and will push you up? Secondly, you get to be as creative as you want in growing and developing your enterprise. There are basically no limits to how innovative you can be. There is no stifling of your marketing talents or novel ideas. How often do you get to do this at a job? My guess is not often at all because there would be no real reason to. Thirdly, only an employer can determine what he gets paid or what he's worth. In your own business, you get to determine what you get paid and what you are worth . . . no one else. When you embrace the employer mentality you will see your self worth and personal stock rise in value. This will affect your confidence and as a result, the attainment of your goals and dreams.

One last point, as any employer or business owner will tell you, they take their enterprise seriously and not as a part time hobby. The employee-minded new associate who treats his or her business the same will find that their approach will be that of a part time hobby and not give it the respect and seriousness it demands. To tackle your new business opportunity or sales profession with anything less than an employer-minded weightiness will cause you to dilute the potential of the opportunity and the results you signed up for. Your survival depends on this all too important transition of thought, behavior, and attitude.

## How can I apply this Chapter to my business?

_____

_____

_____

_____

_____

_____

_____

_____

_____

_____

_____

_____

_____

_____

_____

_____

_____

# CHAPTER 8

*"Experience is not what happens to a man; it is what a man does with what happens to him."*

Aldous Huxley

## "THE POSSIBILITIES NOT THE PERSON"

John was not looking for opportunity but was willing to give his best friend a few minutes to share what he was so excited about. The last thing on John's mind was to join anything, let alone a business. Nevertheless, as any good friend will do at times, he offered himself up to be a guinea pig for his friend's new venture. As it turned out, within a few minutes of hearing his friend's rendition of the business presentation, John was hooked. It all made sense to him and he thought that he would be a fool not to at least give the opportunity a test drive. So, he got signed up, pumped up, and dreamed up. The more John studied his business model, the product, the marketing, and the compensation the more eager he was to get his business off and running. This once indifferent person was now thrilled to see the possibilities of his opportunity take shape. The concept of building a team of like-minded entrepreneurs and receiving passive income as a result of their efforts was the highlight for him. He envisioned developing a huge organization. John followed the business and marketing plan to precision, memorized scripts, utilized the training resources available, wrote his goals out and read them everyday, and posted dream pictures on a large corkboard. There was no question he was totally sold out to the company, concepts, and building a big organization with a lot of people. He talked to people daily and recruited a decent number of new associates on his team. John was well on his way. So, why did he barely last 5 months before throwing in the proverbial towel? What happened that led him to give up so soon? This vibrant individual who seemed to be on the fast track to stardom didn't even make it to his own 30 yard line before forfeiting the game and leaving the stadium entirely. I know that there are many Johns out there. You may be one yourself or you have worked with them in the past. Whichever the case, the answer to this mystery is one that I have, over the years, observed in others and in myself as well. Unfortunately, no one ever told John that people will let you down and in a business that requires hopeful expectations of people, it is easy to get discouraged when those expectations never materialize. John poured out his heart in believing in each person he introduced into the business. He focused on that new business partner as being the one to take him to the Promised Land. His emphasis leaned heavy on that one individual who seemed to have the qualities of a future business champion. He practiced this with just about every person that joined his business. With each new person he leveled inflated expectations on them. In other words, he would put all his eggs in that basket. With behavior like this, it was no surprise that John eventually quit after most of his people let him down. His bubble burst and so went his drive, enthusiasm, and interest. John was truly blindsided due to naiveté and gullibility about the nature of people.

This point is worth repeating and you accepting. People will let you down. Period. It's just the way it is. Unfortunately, it is human nature to fall short many times. Your expectations of what you believe a person can deliver may not always come to pass (if it does at all), to the degree of intensity, productivity, and speed of development that you hoped for. Therefore, learn to channel your focus, excitement, and hopeful expectations on the possibilities and not the actual person. The endless possibilities that can become realities through the efforts of that person are the aspect to get most enthusiastic about. The interesting thing about this dynamic is that if the possibilities fail to manifest then the letdown is not so hard to swallow because, by the very nature of a possibility, you are aware (conscious or not) that it may or may not work. It is easier to survive through numerous, unrealized possibilities than it is numerous, unrealized expectations of one person after another. A person letting you down is a much harder experience to forget or get over. Too many letdowns like that become too painful and very soon thereafter, unbearable. The result is what most will do to avoid the pain. They quit the task. Let me give you another example with different context so that you can fully understand this point.

My first car was a used Dodge Aries which my father bought for me to drive him and my mother around on occasion as well as commute back and forth to college. Since neither of them drove, he figured it would serve both purposes. Now, if anyone remembers those cars, they were not the best quality cars yet got the job done. When the car finally gave out, was I devasted? Absolutely not! I knew that the car was just the method of transportation; it was where the car would take me that was important and exciting. The possibilities that existed by having that car was the true focus. It was the joy in driving my parents around that mattered. It was the getting me back and forth to college to receive my education. It was the wonderful dates that I was able to go on. The fact that it was a Dodge Aries was not relevant. However, the promise of where it could take me was. By the way, when the car broke down I got another one; a used white T-Top Chevy IROC. Guess what, it also took me places where I had wonderful experiences. Oh, yes and when that one finally broke down, I got something else. Imagine, for a second, if I had put so much weight and emphasis on the Dodge Aries that after it broke down and did not operate properly or effectively anymore, I would have declared the auto industry worthless, the driving experience overrated, and would have given up my driving license altogether. Ridiculous, right? I didn't channel all of my enthusiasm into any one car because cars eventually break down due to wear and tear but that was not going to stop me from driving. Comparably, people in your business will also disappoint you at times. They will quit or fall way short of your expectations. It is part of the business. Don't get caught up on the person but the possibilities that the person brings with them.

I was at a recent training conference and a once notable recruiter had a chance to address the audience. He began to explain why he turned his focus away from the very aspect of the business that enticed early on, the ability and privilege to build an organization, and focus on personal production. As I sat there and heard him give his rationale I recognized his dilemma. It occurred to me that if a seasoned business builder can fall prey to this emotional trap then new people don't stand a chance unless they are forewarned. It is the same trap that escorted John out of a promising start so early on. It is the same trap that any leader at any level can still succumb to. The only difference is that well equipped and battle tested leaders can overcome and escape the trap easily. They can immediately rebound. A new person very often does not and it costs them their possibilities of winning. My last thought on this very vital survival tip is that the possibilities  for where your business will take you through the building of an organization should merit your energy and total focus. It is where you must draw your confidence and fortitude if you are to survive your business long enough to build one.

## How can I apply this Chapter to my business?

_____

_____

_____

_____

_____

_____

_____

_____

_____

_____

_____

_____

_____

_____

_____

# CHAPTER 9

*"Don't dodge difficulties: meet them, greet them, beat them. All great men have been through the wringer."*

A.A. Milne

## "DISCIPLINE YOUR DISAPPOINTMENTS"

In the real world things do not always work out they way we would like them to. Even the best laid plans can find their demise. Flawless strategies followed through with perfect execution still do not guarantee the results you seek. It is a sad and unfortunate reality of life that, at times, things just will not go right even after you have done all you can do. As a result, disappointment can be par for the course for any success-seeking dreamer. Experiencing disappointment is not the issue. It comes with the territory. The issue is how you deal with it. Allowing your disappointment to distract you or sway you from your goals or frequently giving in to disappointments will only lead to discouragement and soon thereby, the exit door. As I list in this book the top ten survival points, I am drawn to this one as probably the most crucial and, not only relevant to your business, but I find to life in general. This lesson is applicable to many areas of life. Prioritizing how to discipline your disappointments should be one of your primary concerns because lack thereof will become a stumbling block to your growth, professionally and personally, for a number of reasons. First, unbridled disappointment can throw your convictions about your decision to get started awry. There is no way that you can keep your eyes on the road ahead if you continually shift your focus to the rear view mirrors. It's an accident waiting to happen. Similarly, not handling your discouragements properly will cause you to look back often and question whether you made the right decision. It's an accident waiting to happen. Secondly, they can cause you to doubt yourself and your ability as a business owner, a leader, a recruiter, a sales person, and a professional. When I first got started, I was 21 years old and had zero professional experience in financial services. I was a social worker, a personal trainer, a former bodybuilder, an entertainer, and I bounced at the night clubs for extra cash when everything else was slow. I know all about doubting yourself and questioning whether you fit in. After most of my friends, family, and co-workers shunned me, I doubted whether I could do it. However, my doubt was overshadowed by my deliberation and determination that I would make it work no matter what. I was able to discipline my disappointments many times over. I still work on that till this day but the battles are far, few and futile. Thirdly, when setbacks are not appropriately handled, then the blame game begins. This is when everyone else and everything else is to blame for you not progressing in your business as you would like. At this point, it's the manager, the company, the products, the company website, the people on your team, the paperwork, the tests or certifications, the compensation plan, the weather, the economy, the demographics, the "baby momma drama", and on and on. Unfortunately, this seems to be the first real sign that the exit door is in clear sight for that person. Now, this may seem like a cruel statement but time usually affirms its truth. Lastly, when you don't regulate your frustrations, a sense of panic and fear can seep into your mental amour and wreak havoc on your confidence and decision making process. All it takes is a little panic and fear and the most stable of persons can be thrown into a frenzy especially if business and financial progress is not yet consistently growing. I have seen many associates over the years ditch a marketing plan that works and strike out on creating their own plan only to find that it failed miserably and soon thereafter they have either quit their business or have come back to the original company model in place. The lack of monitoring their discouragements had become the culprit to their irrational actions and served only to delay their advancement.

Any great leader, coach, pastor, sales manager, or teacher who has been at their post for a number of years can provide you ample accounts of individuals who displayed amazing promise and talent that either never quite made it to their potential or struggled with many starts and stops along the way. This is because they never handled disappointment well. The crash course was never attended or given, for that matter, so with one let down after another, this great candidate lost the drive to continue and "died" along the way. This may be you at this very moment. In the quietness of your solitude, you are being slaughtered by discouragement and are almost about to give up. This would be an awful shame because there is so much that you can still accomplish with a change of focus and discipline. If

I may, I'd like to share with you a few helpful directives that may become your life line.

Discipline first begins with understanding that the world will not end if someone you invite does not show up or cancels business. Discipline also means that you comprehend that the world does not revolve around your schedule so just because you are ready and available to meet with someone does not mean that they are available and ready to meet with you. Granting someone grace and exercising patience is essential. Furthermore, discipline means that you come to the realization that for the many who disappoint you, there are countless others that delight you. It's all part of the checks and balances of the business universe. Sometimes those you expect will delight you only disappoint you while those who you thought would surely disappoint you become your most unexpected and surprising delight! I know that most people who make decisions to join a business opportunity do it because they are ambitious, dissatisfied, yet hopeful dreamers. Along with that comes a higher level of desire and willingness to sacrifice than most people ever possess. So, with this particular group can also come the highest level of disappointment. It's only natural that as the level of purpose and aspiration of someone increases so does the potential for let down when things don't go the way they planned. I can attest to this first hand. I believe any honest person will confess this also. Therefore, it is not wrong or weak minded to be disappointed or disheartened when things don't go right. In fact, discouragement gets the first right of refusal when you fail an exam, when your best person quits, when the client calls and has changed her mind, when nobody will give you the time of day, when your family thinks you're crazy, when your calendar has more cancellations than confirmations, and so on. It's only natural to get frustrated and upset. After all, you are only trying to do something special with your life. You are only human. By the way, anybody that tells you otherwise does not live on planet Earth or is some super anomaly, freak of nature that never struggles with this emotion. The key is and always will be how you deal with it. For everyone, this will be different. Nonetheless, the common denominator has to be that your determination becomes greater than your disappointments. Defy your discouragements with resolve and you'll have afforded yourself a chance to thrive. Finally, if nothing else, exercise the timeless method to handling your disappointments: The 4 "Its" . . .

**GET OVER IT! MOVE ON WITH IT! DEAL WITH IT! SNAP OUT OF IT!**

## How can I apply this Chapter to my business?

_____

_____

_____

_____

_____

_____

_____

_____

_____

_____

_____

_____

_____

_____

_____

_____

# CHAPTER 10

*"Genius is 1 percent inspiration and 99 percent perspiration."*

Thomas Edison

## "RECOGNIZE THE FLUKES"

Overnight success is a fluke. Every business boasts of that incredible person that skyrockets to the top in almost overnight fashion. That individual is virtually non-existent then within a matter of a relatively short time span their business has catapulted to the level of success that few ever get to experience or only after years of grinding it out. It seems like an effortless climb to the proverbial top. You could almost categorize that person as wholly anointed for success. They receive stellar recognition, grow huge teams, produce ridiculous business, and enjoy dreamlike income. Well, that sort of meteoric rise to the top is a fluke. Meaning, it is not suppose to happen that way. Although the person himself is not a fluke, and they deserve every bit of the spoils of success because at some point they made the decision to begin building their business, it's their seemingly untested, unfettered, and effortless rise to the top that is. That being said, you and I would love to have many individuals like this in our businesses but the reality is that it is highly unlikely. The quicker you grasp this the less you will find yourself comparing your possibly slow moving business to those individuals. Over the years, I have always sought to find why some people quit and why some stay. It is a fascination of mine to learn more so that I can help more people stay. My hard drawn conclusion is that some people will stay and some will go. How's that for intellectual discovery? It's just the way it is. This will never change. It's nature. There is no rhyme or reason. One day, if I get my own planet, I'll rearrange the deal but for now, it is what it is. Yet, I cannot just sit idly by and settle for doing nothing so I decided years ago to inquire about this phenomena because that's what you do when you want to get better, you seek wisdom and understanding. I wanted to find out what were some of the underlying reasons why people would not only quit my business, but other businesses as well. I even spoke to other leaders from other business opportunities, organizations, and sales companies. What I found was what I suspected and the purpose for this particular chapter. A small percentage of people did not get past the initial phase of building their business because they often compared their progress to those with meteoric rise. They modeled their progress and standards to that of someone with overnight success and when they did not see it coming to pass that way they felt hopeless, inadequate, and a failure. Well, it was not surprising that some would quit their opportunity due to carrying these heavy, burdensome expectations. If you find yourself comparing your business development to that of a fluke then your career may be short lived.

Now, if I have deflated your bubble then I might have just saved your business because surviving means living and working in the realm of reality and not the whimsical. Let me be crystal clear on this, you have to dream, absolutely. It is an integral part of fighting the good fight in your business development but not to the extent that you take up residence in dream land and not deal with reality. In this matter, reality dictates that your upward business progression and success journey is supposed to be laden with setbacks, challenges, mistakes, and often times, startover's. Your weathered struggle becomes the testimony that inspires others to keep going. More people can relate to the one who was battletested than the one who was able to skate by without a scratch. This is the rule. Anything else is an exception to it. Andrew Carnegie is well known for saying, "Anything in life worth having is worth working for!" Probably, one of the disadvantages of new people not recognizing the flukes is that they believe that that's the way it is suppose to happen for everyone. Everyone is suppose to recruit massive amounts of people, produce outrageous sales numbers, get promoted to the top executive levels, open up multiple offices, become a great presenter and speaker, quit their job and go full time, be on the cover of the company or trade publication or website, and oh yes, walk on water all within months of joining. Let me reiterate to you, my friend, this is not the way it works. It is not reality. You probably will not recruit massive amounts of people early on, produce outrageous numbers in sales, get executive level promotions, open up multiple offices (let alone one), become a great speaker or presenter, you won't be firing your boss anytime soon, your "made for radio face" will not grace the cover of your company magazine or the website homepage either, and forget about walking on water (that feat has already been done by someone) within a couple of months. Does this mean, you can't still win big in your business? No. Does it mean that you shouldn't try to become the fluke yourself? No. Does it mean that you may not introduce the next fluke story into the chronicles of your company's history? No. Anything is possible to all of the above. What it means is that if you don't do any of the above, it is no reason to die. You can still survive and thrive. My mentor in business will tell you that he was pretty darn awful when he joined our current company. He often reminds us that it took him six months to recruit one person (the best was ten in his first year), over a year to start making decent money, over a year to get a promotion, a number of years to open his own office yet through perseverance and commitment he has amassed quite a significant operation over 25 years that spans the US and Canada with over 100 offices and over 100 executive level promotions in his organization. His organization produces more financial business yearly than small companies. His annual income consistently soars over a million a year; he has become a legend in our company and in certain parts of the financial services industry as well. By no means an overnight success, but one by which to admire and respect. In another instance, recently I attended our company's annual convention and had a chance to see and hear from some of the new rising stars. I was particularly impressed with one leader whom I had never heard of before because she did not appear in any of the recent events, contests, leader's bulletins, website, etc. Due to her business performance, she was receiving a lot of recognition and when given an opportunity to speak she began to share her journey with this company which started for her in 2004. Needless to say, as I listened to her humble beginnings and unassuming story, I could sense how many in that crowd of 20,000 were relating to her story. After seven consistent, yet somewhat inconspicuous years, she is now starting to hit her stride and getting national recognition. Hardly an overnight success, but nevertheless an aspiring business example to model. If your goal is to find business heroes to be encouraged by, then find those whose starts were not pretty and maybe a bit obscure; those who can share a common theme with you . . . one of true persistency through the difficult times as well as the easy times; those who can provide a true source of encouragement and motivation which comes from a grassroots understanding of the process. The flukes serve to prove that anything is possible which is great news, but your survival will be enhanced when you channel your efforts on the inescapable long road to the top.

## How can I apply this Chapter to my business?

_____

_____

_____

_____

_____

_____

_____

_____

_____

_____

_____

_____

_____

_____

_____

_____

# CONCLUSION

It is my earnest desire that you take to heart what these previous chapters have revealed to you. Although, there are many more (equally as important) topics that I could have included, I felt that these ten were priority to begin with. Nevertheless, they are too important not to adhere to. It is my conviction and experience that the survival of your involvement in your business depends on your awareness and execution of these survival tips. Look people, the reality is that you never know who you may introduce into your business, if you stay around long enough, who can change your family's future forever. There are countless legitimate examples of such cases among every single business opportunity out there. By the way, this is not just subject to our industry alone. It also happens in any sales company that has an element of recruiting new talent. Every single one of them can boast of numerous examples to confirm this truth. The fact is there is an unknown superstar out there in the making that is supposed to be introduced to your business by you. Then again, your early departure due to your inability to survive will never see that come to pass. In the same way, there is a client in real need that has been assigned to you but will never benefit from your product or service because you gave up too soon. Still, you have a dream life awaiting you but you have to hang around long enough to enjoy it as it manifests.

One of my favorite Scripture verses can be found in Deuteronomy 8:18. It reconciles that the ability to get wealth or create wealth is given to you by God. I've checked just about every Bible version and translation of this particular verse and they all render the same message. What I have extracted from this is good news for all of us as well because the verse does not say a chosen few, the super smart, the incredibly gifted, the college graduate, the PhD candidate, the black, the white, the brown nor yellow, the good looking or not good looking, the bald, or with full head of hair, the New Yorker or Londoner, young or old, the Scripture is impartial. It includes not only the hearer of that day but everyone today as well. This means YOU. You have been humbly equipped by God with every ability possible to create the prosperous life that you desire. You have not been shortchanged of anything necessary for you to achieve greatness. It's already been deposited in you. Your DNA carries the gene of success and all you have to do is relentlessly pursue its development with heart, discipline, wisdom, and tenacious focus. If you do, then your impact story will one day be proudly told by your family for generations to come. It will be the stuff that business success stories are made of. Oh yes, my friends, there is much riding on you seeing your opportunity through, for all that its worth, and achieving success. Decide right now that no matter what the challenge . . . no matter what the setback . . . no matter who let's you down . . . no matter the battle, you WILL survive. You WILL thrive. So, that one day, you WILL arrive at your appointed place of victory! (Somebody shout AMEN!)

# CONTACT AND BOOKING INFORMATION

Visit our website www.SurvivetoThriveGuide.com

Email Jay Maymi at survivetothrive@ymail.com

For speaking engagement requests and book signings, email booking_survivetothrive@ymail.com

 www.facebook.com/
survivetothriveguide

 www.linkedin.com/in/jaymaymi

 @jaymaymi